WHERE on EARTH?

COASTLINES

Discover Earth's amazing places

Susie Brooks

WAYLAND
www.waylandbooks.co.uk

Published in paperback in 2018 by Wayland
Copyright © Hodder and Stoughton, 2015

Editor: Elizabeth Brent
Designer: Rocket Design (East Anglia) Ltd

ISBN   978 0 7502 9069 2
eBook ISBN   978 0 7502 9068 5

Printed in China

10 9 8 7 6 5 4 3 2 1

Pictures by Shutterstock except: Cover: Nancy Rose/Getty Images; p4 (top): Getty Images; p5 (top): Tony Waltham/
Getty Images, (whole spread): Stefan Chabluk; p8 (top): AFLO / MAINICHI NEWSPAPER/epa/Corbis; p11 (top): Streeta
Lecker/Getty Images, (right): YONHAP NEWS AGENCY/epa/Corbis; p12 (top): Rafael Maestri Righes/Getty Images;
p13 (top right): Matt Cardy/Getty Images, (bottom left): Panoramic Images/Getty Images; p14 (top): Erhard Nerger/
imageBROKER/Corbis, (bottom): Stefan Chabluk; p15 (top): Nicolas Thibaut/Getty Images; p16 (top): airyuhi/a.
collectionRF/Getty Images; p17 (top): UniversalImagesGroup/Getty Images, (middle): DavidCallan/iStock; p20: The
Asahi Shimbun/Getty Images; p21 (top): Associated Newspapers/REX, (middle): George Steinmetz/Corbis, (bottom
right): Planet Observer/UIG, (bottom left): Geoff Renner/Robert Harding World Imagery/Corbis; p22 (top): Stocktrek
Images/Getty Images, (bottom): Visuals Unlimited, Inc./Wim van Egmond; p23 (top left): Sonke Johnsen/Visuals
Unlimited/Corbis, (top right): David Shale/Nature Picture Library/Corbis; p24 (bottom): David Doubilet/Getty Images;
p27 (top): Stefan Chabluk, (middle): Shafiqul Alam/Demotix/Corbis; p29 (middle left): STR/AFP/Getty Images, (middle
right): Emily Riddell/Getty Images

The website addresses (URLs) included in this book were valid at the time of going to press. However,
it is possible that contents or addresses may have changed since the publication of this book.
No responsibility for any such changes can be accepted by either the author or the Publisher.

Wayland, an imprint of Hachette Children's Group
Part of Hodder & Stoughton
Carmelite House
50 Victoria Embankment
London
EC4Y 0DZ

An Hachette UK Company
www.hachette.co.uk
www.hachettechildrens.co.uk

CONTENTS

Where on Earth are coasts?

Earth is covered in land and sea – and where the two meet, that's a coast! Some coasts are huge, fringing whole continents, while others surround islands you could cross in a few steps. If you've ever run on a beach or paddled in the sea, you've been to a coast.

All around the globe, people live and work by coasts or go there on their holidays. In this book you'll discover WHERE, HOW and WHY ON EARTH these edgy places shape our world.

LONG WALK

Canada has the longest coastline of any country. If you walked the Canadian shores covering 20km a day, it would take you 27 years!

BIG BAY

A bay is a place where the coast curves inwards. The bay with the longest shoreline is Canada's Hudson Bay, at 12,268km.

SEASIDE CITIES

Many of the world's biggest cities, including Tokyo, Shanghai and New York (below), have grown up next to coasts. They're ideally placed here for shipping and trade.

WATER WORLD

From space, Earth looks mainly blue – because oceans cover more than two-thirds of the planet!

LOCKED IN

Some countries are landlocked, meaning they don't have a coast at all.

CRUMBLING COASTLINES

Coasts are always changing as water interacts with the land. In some places, cliffs are wearing away by several metres a year.

500,000,000-PEOPLE LONG

Coastlines are hard to measure, but they add up to over a million kilometres worldwide. Straightened out, they would wrap at least 25 times round the Equator. That's the same as more than half a billion adults lying down head to toe!

TOP 10 LONGEST COASTLINES (km)

1. CANADA 202,080
2. INDONESIA 54,716
3. GREENLAND 44,087
4. RUSSIA 37,653
5. THE PHILIPPINES 36,289
6. JAPAN 29,751
7. AUSTRALIA 25,760
8. NORWAY 25,148
9. UNITED STATES 19,924
10. NEW ZEALAND 15,134

SURROUNDED!

A peninsula is land surrounded by water on three sides.

SHIPWRECKED

The Skeleton Coast in Namibia got its spooky name from piles of bones left by the whaling industry. It's also the site of thousands of deadly shipwrecks, caused by blinding fog.

SANDY LAND

When waves dump sand and other sediment at coasts, they can build up new land. That's how beaches grow!

What gives coasts their crooked shape?

If you look at a map of the land and sea, you won't see many smooth edges. Our coasts are bashed by waves, jiggled by Earth forces and battered by the weather all the time. No wonder the land gives way in places, creating a jagged outline.

The biggest land shapes (our continents) formed many millions of years ago. Huge sections of Earth's crust, called plates, very slowly moved and broke up the land. Today the plates are still moving and jostling, tugging the continents in different directions. If you took a trip far into the future, the world could look very different again!

Guanabara Bay in Rio de Janeiro, Brazil, was bashed into shape by the Atlantic Ocean.

NOTES ON EROSION

Some rock is harder and resists erosion, leaving headlands jutting into the water.

SOME PLATES MOVE BY JUST 2.5CM EACH YEAR; OTHERS SHIFT BY 15CM – THE SPEED YOUR HAIR GROWS!

RIP!

The 'supercontinent' Pangaea formed about 300 million years ago, then began to break up after about 100 million years. The water in Earth's oceans moved to fill in the gaps.

Look at the outlines of South America and Africa – you can see they once fitted together.

250 million years ago

200 million years ago

145 million years ago

65 million years ago

Present day

BASH!

When the power of the sea wears land away, this is called erosion. It can form all sorts of dents in the coastline, from tiny caves to gigantic bays.

Headland

Bay

Sea cave

Arch

These columns are called stacks

FREEZE

Fjords create the most crooked coastlines ever. These deep, narrow inlets were carved by glaciers (slow-moving rivers of ice) during long frozen periods, called ice ages.

Norway is only 1,750km long, but its fjord-cut coastline wiggles in and out for an amazing 25,148km!

Sognefjord, the longest inlet in Norway, stretches for more than 203km. That's nothing compared to Greenland's Scoresby Sund – at 350km, it would reach from London to Paris!

Where are the world's biggest waves?

It depends where you're looking. Scientists have discovered waves of up to 244m (taller than some skyscrapers) *underneath* the sea! Underwater waves look the same as the water around them, but they are a different temperature or have a different level of salt.

A devastating tsunami wave sweeps ashore in Japan in 2011.

Ocean waves aren't born big and bad. They get whipped up by winds out at sea and grow taller as they reach shallow waters close to land. As a wave nears the shore, water at the back of it travels faster than the front – until eventually the wave topples, or breaks.

The deadliest waves are called tsunamis and they are shaken into action by earthquakes, landslides or volcanoes. Tsunamis are giant walls of water which can crash several kilometres inland. They can move as fast as a jet plane and wipe out buildings and anything else in their path.

WAVE FORMATION

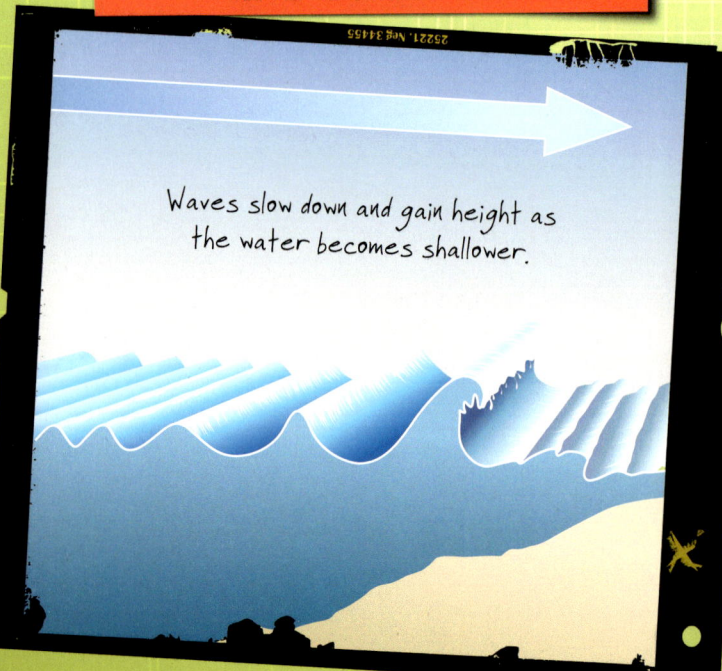

Waves slow down and gain height as the water becomes shallower.

MONSTER WAVES!

BIGGEST OCEAN WAVE: 34m

This was reported by officers of the US Navy oil ship USS Ramapo in the North Pacific on 7 February, 1933. Luckily, they lived to tell the tale!

BIGGEST WAVE SURFED: 30m

Both Garrett McNamara and his friend Carlos Brune claim to have ridden 30m waves off the coast of Nazaré, Portugal, in 2013. The official record, set by McNamara in the same place in 2011, is 23.8m.

Either way, they'd tower over the tallest known dinosaur with its neck at full stretch!

BIGGEST TSUNAMI WAVE: 524m

Triggered by an earthquake and landslide in Alaska's Lituya Bay in 1958, this monster uprooted trees over 500m above sea level (higher than the Empire State Building).

DEADLIEST WAVE KNOWN: 230,000 people killed

The Indian Ocean tsunami of 2004 affected 14 countries. Its waves reached speeds of 800kph, heights of 10m and slammed up to 2km inland.

THE WAVES YOU SEE BREAKING ON A BEACH COULD HAVE TRAVELLED FOR THOUSANDS OF KILOMETRES!

THE RECORD FOR THE MOST SURFERS RIDING THE SAME WAVE AT ONCE IS 110!

What makes the tide go in and out?

Next time the sea creeps up the beach and steals your flip-flops, blame it on outer space! Tides rise and fall (or move in and out) twice a day in most places. Believe it or not, this motion of the ocean is mainly the Moon's fault.

The Moon travels in a loop around Earth, and creates a force called gravity. This force tugs at our oceans and makes them bulge out. Where the bulge happens, you'll find a high tide; elsewhere the tide is low. As the Moon keeps moving (and Earth keeps spinning), the ocean bulge moves too.

Even the Sun joins in with the tugging! The strongest tides, called spring tides, happen twice a month when the Earth, Sun and Moon are all in line. The weakest tides, called neap tides, take place twice monthly when the Moon and Sun are at right angles.

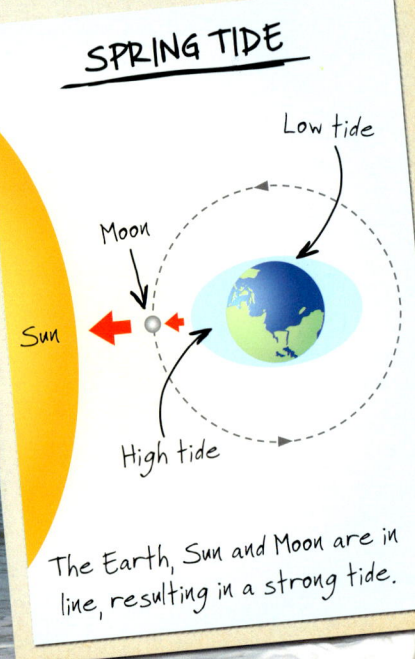

SPRING TIDE

Low tide

Moon

Sun

High tide

The Earth, Sun and Moon are in line, resulting in a strong tide.

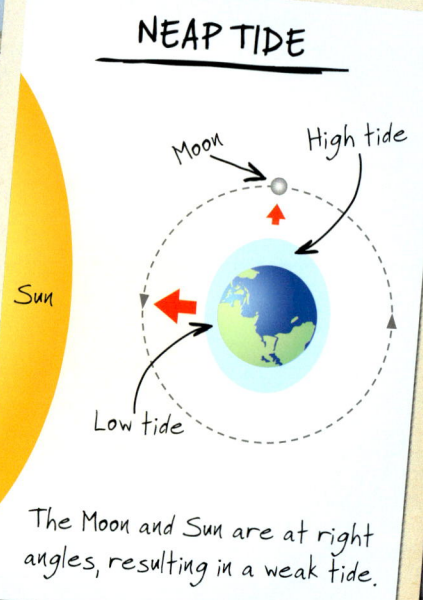

NEAP TIDE

Moon

High tide

Sun

Low tide

The Moon and Sun are at right angles, resulting in a weak tide.

TIDE NOTES

HIGH-RISE

Tidal range is the difference between high and low tide. The most extreme is in the Bay of Fundy, Canada, where the sea rises and falls by up to 16m - enough to cover a five-storey building!

At high tide, the sea rushes into rivers and pushes their flow backwards. This is called a tidal bore. Some tidal bores are very popular with surfers and white-water rafters!

BIG BORE

The world's biggest tidal bore happens on the Qiantang river in China, where waves reach up to 9m!

LOW-RANGE

Small seas, such as the Mediterranean, have tidal ranges of less than a metre.

EARTH SHAPER

The same forces that cause tides in the oceans affect the Earth, stretching it into a slight oval shape!

TIDAL POWER

In some places, scientists harness the power of the tide by directing the water through turbines to create electricity.

Where is the world's longest beach?

If you tried to walk the length of Praia do Cassino in Brazil, it would take at least two days and two nights! Stretching from the city of Rio Grande all the way to Brazil's border with Paraguay, this chart-topping beach is close to 250km long. That's a lot of potential for building sandcastles.

Sand is basically ground-down rock, pounded into tiny pieces by rivers and the sea. When waves keep dumping it on a flat piece of land, it builds up to form a beach. Beaches come in many shapes and sizes and are always changing as waves bring new materials and take away others.

Some beaches are made of pebbles, or shingle. These tend to be built by high-energy waves and are steeper than sandy beaches. If an area is home to enough shelled sea creatures, beaches can be covered in shells that wash up when they die.

TOP FIVE LONGEST BEACHES

Praia do Cassino, Brazil 250km

Cox's Bazaar, India 241km

Padre Island, Texas, USA 209km

Ninety Mile Beach, Australia 145km

Ninety Mile Beach, New Zealand 141.5km

Shell Beach in Western Australia is over 120km long and made up of billions of tiny cockle shells that go 10m deep. The cockles cluster here because the sea is super-salty, which suits them but not their predators!

STRANGE SANDS

Most sand is made of a mineral called quartz, but there are some surprises too...

LAVA is volcanic rock that usually makes jet-black sand. A few volcanic beaches are green – from a mineral in some lava, called olivine!

DIAMONDS have been mined for years on beaches in Namibia, Africa. Other gems, such as sapphires, emeralds and garnets, are found around the world as grains of sand.

PARROTFISH POO – yes, much of the fine white sand on coral beaches comes from coral that's been eaten and digested by parrotfish!

SANDY SLEEP

In 2008, the world's first sand hotel was built on a beach in Dorset, England. It had no roof, no bathrooms and disappeared as soon as it rained!

SEASONAL SIZE

Beaches tend to be wider in summer when the waves are gentle. Stormy winter waves sweep more sand away from the beach.

SAND ISLAND

Fraser Island, off the coast of Queensland, Australia, is the largest sand island in the world. About half a million tourists visit it every year.

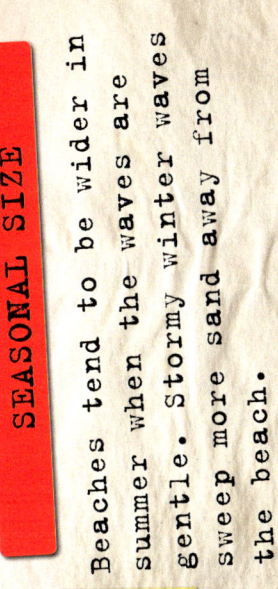

Where can you find a giant spit?

This isn't as yucky as it sounds. A spit is a long strip of sand or shingle that juts into the sea, with one end joined to the land. A gigantic example is the Curonian Spit, on the border of Russia and Lithuania. It's 98km long and has been lived on since prehistoric times.

SOME DUNES ON THE CURONIAN SPIT REACH UP TO 60M HIGH!

HOW SPITS FORM

The spit forms in calm, shallow water.

Winds blow sand along the coast.

Spits form when winds blow at an angle to the coastline. Waves carry material in a zig-zag motion along the beach, piling it up at one end. Over time, a spit can grow a hook if the wind direction changes further out at sea. Sometimes a spit links an island to the mainland — then it's called a tombolo.

The Curonian Spit has been thrashed by the wind and waves for 5,000 years! Huge, shifting sand dunes have built up on it, and at times even buried whole villages. Now the spit is protected and woodland covers much of its surface area. The vegetation helps to lock the dunes in place.

DUNE GIANTS

The tallest coastal sand dune in the world is Mount Tempest, on Australia's Moreton Island. At 280m, it's nearly as high as the Eiffel Tower.

Europe's highest sand dune is the Dune of Pilat in France, rising up to 117m above sea level. It's 3km long, 500m wide and contains about 60 million cubic metres of sand - enough to fill 24,000 Olympic pools!

DESERT HEIGHTS

The biggest sand dunes are in deserts - they make Mount Tempest look quite small!

Cerro Blanco, Nazca Valley, Peru: 1,176m

Cerro Medanoso, Atacama desert, Chile: 550m

Bilutu Peak, Badain Jaran desert, China: 500m

Rig-e Yalan, Dasht-e Lut desert, Iran: 470m

Isaouane-n-Tifernine sand sea, Sahara desert, Algeria: 465m

NOTES ON DUNES

WALKERS

Many sand dunes 'walk'. When winds blow at dunes, they take sand off the near side and dump it on the far side. This makes the dunes slowly shift along.

DUNE TUNES

Some dunes whistle, sing, hum or even boom. The sound is made when the top layer of sand is whipped off by the wind.

On massive dunes, the rumble can reach 105 decibels - nearly as loud as a pop concert!

What happens when a river meets the sea?

Most major rivers carry their water on a one-way trip to the seaside. When they get there, they also offload all the bits of land that they've picked up. Every day, rivers dump up to 55 million tonnes (about 7 million elephants!) of rock, mud and sand into the ocean.

An estuary is a place where fresh water from a river mixes with the salty sea. The name for this coastal cocktail is 'brackish water'. All sorts of habitats are found here, from mudflats and marshlands to sandbanks and mangrove swamps (see p26).

Many types of animal nest, breed and feed in estuaries. The estuarine crocodile is the world's biggest reptile, with big jaws and big teeth to match. These are also popular places for people. Of the 32 largest cities in the world, 22 are built on estuaries!

The vast city of Tokyo was originally known as Edo, meaning 'estuary'!

ESTUARIES ARE THE NURSERY GROUNDS FOR TWO-THIRDS OF THE FISH AND SHELLFISH WE EAT.

The massive jaws of the estuarine croc.

Wading birds with long legs, long beaks and long toes find walking on and feeding in the mud easy!

DELTA NOTES

DELTAS

If the tide can't wash away all the sediment dumped by a river, new land called a delta builds up. Many deltas are so big that millions of people live on them.

Lots of small river channels cut through a delta plain.

✳ Deltas were named for their triangular shape, which look like the Greek letter delta!

✳ Delta soil is rich and ideal for farming. About 40 million people in Egypt live on the Nile river delta, and two-thirds of the country's crops are produced there. ➤

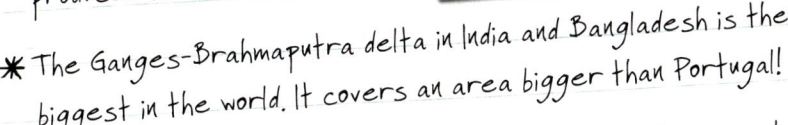

✳ The Ganges-Brahmaputra delta in India and Bangladesh is the biggest in the world. It covers an area bigger than Portugal!

✳ Deltas can grow as rivers bring more sediment. They can also shrink from erosion or rising sea levels.

WHY IS THE SEA SO SALTY?

Rivers pick up tiny amounts of mineral salts from the land and carry them to the sea. But seawater is about 220 times saltier than river water! That's because the Sun's heat makes water evaporate from the massive ocean surface, leaving the salt behind.

If you took out all the salt from the oceans and spread it over the land, it would form a layer more than 150m deep!

Where are the world's highest cliffs?

Picture three Eiffel Towers balanced on top of each other. Then add a Statue of Liberty. They still wouldn't reach the height of the tallest sea cliffs in the world! Found on the Hawaiian island of Molokai, they rise over a kilometre up from the Pacific Ocean.

The cliffs formed about 1.5 million years ago, when a huge chunk of land collapsed into the sea. At the bottom is an isolated peninsula and village, called Kalaupapa. The only way to get there by land is on foot or by mule down a narrow, winding trail. Alternatively, try a helicopter or a boat!

Molokai's giant cliffs are a velvety dark green, draped in vegetation that grows where the waves can't reach. In the wet season you can see spectacular waterfalls pouring down. Because the area is so hard for humans to access, many rare plants and animals live here undisturbed.

THE DRAMATIC CLIFFS OF MOLOKAI ARE FEATURED IN *JURASSIC PARK III*!

CLIFF NOTES

DANGER, DANGER

Cliffs around the world are crumbling and collapsing all the time. The type of rock has a lot to do with it...

✦ The Holderness Coast in England retreats by up to 2m each year, losing around 2 million tonnes of rock. The cliffs are made of soft clay, which erodes easily.

✦ With harder rock, such as limestone, waves can very slowly wear away the bottom of the cliff. If the cliff becomes top-heavy, it collapses.

On the limestone cliffs of Bonifacio, Corsica, people really live on the edge! ➤

FAMOUS

The White Cliffs of Dover, England, are visible from France on a clear day. They're made of chalk, formed from the crushed skeletons of billions of tiny sea creatures.

Ireland's Cliffs of Moher have appeared in several films, including *Harry Potter and the Half-Blood Prince!* Known for their natural beauty, they're one of the country's top tourist sites.

About 30,000 birds live on the Cliffs of Moher.

Can islands appear from nowhere?

By December 2013, the newborn isle had reached the coast of Nishinoshima and joined up with it.

Thanks to undersea volcanoes, yes they can! On 20 November 2013, the world's newest island appeared in the Pacific Ocean off the coast of Japan. It measured about 200m across and popped up near another island, Nishinoshima.

When volcanoes on the seafloor erupt, they can build up mountains of rock. Sometimes these become tall enough to break through the ocean surface. That's what happened with Japan's new island – and it didn't stop there. It kept on growing as the volcano that formed it kept erupting!

At one point, the combined island looked like the cartoon character Snoopy!

NOT ALL NEW ISLANDS SURVIVE. SIMILAR ERUPTIONS AROUND JAPAN HAVE SINCE ERODED AWAY!

By August 2014 the island measured 1.39 square kilometres – over 40 times its original size.

ISLAND NOTES

>>ISLAND SURPRISES<<

- Surtsey emerged off the coast of Iceland in 1963. Eruption followed eruption, and by 1967 the island stood 150m tall. It's now an important nature reserve.

- In 1883, the Indonesian volcano Krakatau destroyed itself in a massive eruption. In 1930, Anak Krakatau ('Child of Krakatau') appeared in its place!

MORE ISLANDS

BIGGEST VOLCANIC ISLAND Iceland is 102,828 square kilometres and 70 million years old.

BIGGEST It's not the largest island of all — that's Greenland, at 2,130,800 square kilometres. Australia is more than three times this size, but it's excluded because it's a continent.

TALLEST The tallest island in the world is New Guinea, rising 4,884m from sea level to its top peak, Puncak Jaya.

LOWEST The Maldives is the lowest island country — just 2.4m above sea level at its highest point.

OLDEST The oldest island is Madagascar, which separated from India about 90 million years ago. It's the fourth-largest island in the world and home to many unique creatures.

LONELIEST The most remote inhabited island group in the world — Tristan da Cunha — is 2,810km from Cape Town, South Africa, and can only be reached (in about six days) by boat!

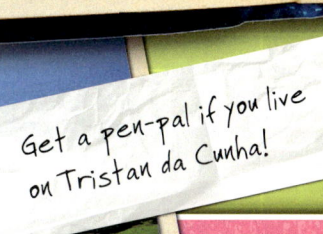

Get a pen-pal if you live on Tristan da Cunha!

Where does a bay glow in the dark?

If you visit certain waters in the dead of night, it's not just the Moon that will light your way. Bioluminescent Bay, on the Puerto Rican island of Vieques, has a natural glow all of its own. It's down to a special type of plankton – tiny organisms that live in the ocean.

When living things give off light, it's called bioluminescence – hence the name of the bay. The sea here is packed with plankton that glow bright blue at night when the water is disturbed. The light is thought to be a 'burglar alarm' system, attracting bigger animals to eat whatever tries to eat the plankton!

Bioluminescent Bay has a narrow opening, meaning that large numbers of the plankton are contained in one place. In fact these living lightbulbs can be seen in oceans around the world. It's sometimes called the milky sea effect.

The sparkly plankton seen through a microscope.

A CUPFUL OF THE BAY'S WATER CONTAINS ABOUT 70,000 GLOWING PLANKTON!

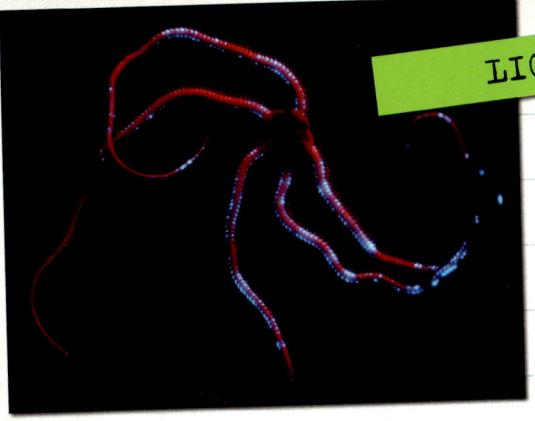

LIGHT UP

BRITTLE STARFISH can shed a glowing limb to put attackers on the wrong track. (A new limb will grow in its place!)

HATCHETFISH adjust their lighting to match their surroundings, as a form of camouflage.

These clever coastal creatures have different methods of survival...

• **BARNACLES** ooze a sticky 'glue' to help them cling to rocks in the roughest surf. They can even hitch a ride on boats, turtles and whales!

• The **MUDSKIPPER** really is a fish out of water. It can walk, eat and breathe on land when the tide goes out.

• The Galápagos **MARINE IGUANA** is the only lizard that survives underwater.

• **HORSESHOE CRABS** look like giant frying pans and have ten eyes each!

• **SEA OTTERS** wrap themselves in kelp growing from the seabed, so they don't drift off while they snooze! They have an unusual ability to eat prickly sea urchins.

Barnacles

Mudskipper

Horseshoe crab

Which coastal creatures can you see from space?

It's actually a whole group of coastal creatures, but Australia's Great Barrier Reef is so huge you could admire it from the Moon! The largest living structure on the planet, it's made up of trillions of coral polyps – invertebrate animals related to jellyfish and sea anemones.

Corals thrive in shallow waters, warmed up by the Sun. Each polyp has a soft body, tentacles and a hard outer skeleton near its base. Thousands of identical polyps live together in colonies, which join together to create a reef. Live coral sits on top of dead coral, and so a reef slowly grows.

The Great Barrier Reef stretches for 2,300km along the Queensland coast and covers an area bigger than Italy. It's made up of about 3,000 smaller reefs and 900 islands, divided by narrow passages. The reef grows by about 2cm per year – the same rate as your fingernails.

REEF NOTES

SOME CORAL COLONIES LOOK LIKE TREES, HONEYCOMB, OR EVEN BRAINS!

A green sea turtle swims off the Great Barrier Reef.

A POLYP MAY BE SMALLER THAN A PINHEAD OR AS BIG AS A PLATE.

HOME!

The Great Barrier Reef is home to about:

* 600 types of coral

* 1,600 species of fish

* 4,000 different molluscs

* 240 types of bird

* plus a massive variety of sponges, anemones, sea worms and other creatures.

Six of the world's seven species of marine turtle live here, as well as many sharks, whales and the dugong - a rare 'sea cow'.

Some reefs in the Great Barrier Reef have more types of fish than the whole Caribbean Ocean!

THREAT

The Crown of Thorns starfish is a threat to coral reefs. A single star can eat 6 square metres of coral a year. Parrotfish are also keen on eating coral (see page 13).

*** TOP 5 LONGEST CORAL REEFS ***

1) Great Barrier Reef (Coral Sea): 2,300km

2) Red Sea Coral Reef (Red Sea): 1,900km

3) New Caledonia Barrier Reef (Pacific Ocean): 1,500km

4) Mesoamerican Barrier Reef (Atlantic Ocean): 943km

5) Florida Reef (Atlantic and Gulf of Mexico): 322km

Which coast is home to killer tigers?

You're usually safe from tigers at the seaside – unless you're exploring the Sundarbans. This huge coastal area of northeast India and Bangladesh is one of the world's biggest mangrove forests. It's the perfect place for killer cats to make their home.

Bengal tigers lurk in the mangroves of the Sundarbans, looking for prey.

Mangrove seeds float in water and can travel long distances.

SUNDARBANS MEANS 'BEAUTIFUL FORESTS'.

Mangroves are trees and shrubs with special roots that have adapted to cope with salty water and changing tides. Found along coasts in warm, tropical areas, they often look as if they're standing on stilts, propped up above the water surface.

Mangrove forests are important because they help to protect the coastline from erosion by storms and tides. They also attract an amazing number of animals… and humans. Around 2.5 million people live in villages surrounding the Sundarbans, fishing and farming the swampy land.

THE SUNDARBANS

MANGROVE VARIETY

Different types of mangrove grow at different levels of the coast, depending on how much salty water they can tolerate.

High tide

Low tide

HUGE HABITAT

The Sundarbans covers around 10,000 square kilometres (over a million football pitches)! About three-fifths of this is in Bangladesh. It's home to more than:

* 315 types of bird * 120 species of fish
* 50 kinds of reptile * 49 different mammals.

Fish and shrimps hide from predators among the mangroves, while tree-climbing crabs and sea snails can shin right up the roots at high tide. The biggest animals include deer, dolphins, rhinoceros – and the only mangrove-dwelling tigers in the world. Hundreds of Bengal tigers live in the Sundarbans.

Deer are on the menu for Bengal tigers.

BENGAL TIGERS

✳ You can hear the roar of a Bengal tiger 3km away!

✳ This killer cat builds several dens and hunts at night, stalking deer, wild boar and other animals.

✳ Bengal tigers usually live alone, and prefer not to share their hunting grounds. Each tiger needs around 50 square kilometres to find enough to eat.

✳ A Bengal tucks into about 30kg of meat (the weight of an average 10-year-old child) every few days.

✳ These tigers can be man-eaters. They attack from behind, so some local people wear backwards-facing masks to try to put them off!

Could the sea swamp a whole city?

People do like to be beside the seaside – so much so that half the world's population lives within 60km of the coast, and three-quarters of all large cities are built there! We use the sea for fishing, shipping goods and having fun. But scientists say sea levels are rising…

Earth's climate has been heating up and cooling down for millions of years, but in the last century it has warmed up quickly. Global warming affects sea levels in two ways:

• When water heats up, it expands – so the oceans need more space.

• Warmer temperatures melt ice sheets and glaciers, making the sea rise higher.

Satellite measurements show that sea levels have been rising by about 3mm a year since the 1990s. According to a recent study, oceans will rise between 0.3 and 1.2m by the end of this century.

The Thames Barrier has been protecting London from flooding for more than 30 years. By 2070, it may need to be replaced.

IN EUROPE, AN ESTIMATED 13 MILLION PEOPLE WOULD BE THREATENED BY A SEA-LEVEL RISE OF 1M.

NOTES ON FLOODS

IF ALL THE ICE MELTED...

...the sea would rise by about 70m – enough to drown hundreds of major cities, and whole countries including the Netherlands and Bangladesh.

The UK would be broken up into many smaller islands.

New York's Statue of Liberty would be waist-deep in water.

RISKY ALREADY

Tsunamis and tropical storms are already a danger to coastal people. Typhoons and hurricanes can swell the sea and cause a storm surge that sweeps fiercely inland.

In 2008, Cyclone Nargis led to extreme coastal flooding in Myanmar, Asia. At least 138,000 people died or went missing.

A cubic metre of water weighs about 1,000kg – the same as a large polar bear. A storm surge can carry thousands of cubic metres per second!

PROTECTION

Cities can protect themselves from flooding by building defences like London's Thames Barrier.

Conserving natural barriers, such as beaches, dunes and mangroves, is important in reducing the damage done by storms and tsunamis.

THE LOW-LYING MALDIVES ISLANDS COULD BE ALMOST COMPLETELY UNDERWATER BY 2100.

What on Earth? words

bay A broad inlet of water where coastal land curves inwards.

brackish Slightly salty.

continent One of Earth's seven major landmasses.

coral reef A mass of underwater organisms called polyps, which build up to form a rocky structure.

crust Earth's rocky surface, made up of continental and oceanic plates.

cyclone A tropical storm. Also known as a hurricane or typhoon in some regions.

delta An area of flat land at the coast, built up by sediment from a river.

dune A hill or ridge of sand, built up by the wind or water.

earthquake Sudden shaking of the ground, caused by plate movements.

Equator An imaginary line around Earth, at equal distance from the North and South Poles.

erosion The wearing away of land by wind, water or other natural processes.

eruption When a volcano ejects lava (molten rock), ash and gas.

estuary A place where one or more rivers flow into the sea.

evaporate To turn from liquid to vapour (gas).

fjord A narrow, deep inlet in the coast between two cliffs.

glacier A slow-moving river of ice, found on high mountains and near the Poles.

gravity A force that pulls physical objects towards each other. When you drop something and it falls, that's Earth's gravity pulling it down. The Sun, Moon and Earth all pull on each other in space.

headland A narrow piece of land that juts out from the coastline into the sea.

ice age An extremely cold period in Earth's history when ice sheets and glaciers spread. The last ice age ended about 11,500 years ago.

islet A very small island.

landslide The collapse of a mass of rock and earth from a mountain, hillside or cliff.

mangrove A type of tree or shrub that grows in coastal swamps, with specially adapted roots that stand above the ground.

plates The jigsaw-like sections of solid rock that together make up Earth's crust.

quartz One of the most common minerals found in Earth's crust.

stack A large column of rock in the sea.

spit A narrow strip of beach-like land that extends out into the sea. It is built up by waves dropping sand or shingle.

storm surge An extreme rise in sea levels caused by a storm.

tidal bore When the incoming tide sends waves up a river, against the direction of the river's flow.

tide The rise and fall in sea levels, usually twice a day in any particular place.

tsunami A huge, destructive sea wave, triggered by an earthquake, volcano or landslide.

Further information

BOOKS

Seas and Oceans (*Our Earth in Action*) by Chris Oxlade, Franklin Watts, 2014

Coastlines Around the World and ***Islands Around the World*** (*Geography Now*) by Jen Green, Wayland, 2012

Rivers Around the World (*Geography Now*) by Jen Green, Wayland, 2011

Coast and Seashores and ***Coral Reefs*** (*Watery Worlds*) by Jinny Johnson, Franklin Watts, 2015

Sailing the Great Barrier Reef (*Travelling Wild*) by Alex Woolf, Wayland, 2013

WEBSITES

www.nationalgeographic.org/encyclopedia/coast/
All about coasts and how they change.

www.onegeology.org/extra/kids/earthprocesses/coasts.html
Find out about waves, tides and more.

www.3dgeography.co.uk/coastal-geography
Facts, info and activities to do with coasts.

www.gbrmpa.gov.au/about-the-reef
The site of Australia's Great Barrier Reef Marine Park Authority.

www.ducksters.com/science/earth_science/ocean_tides.php
The lowdown on tides and why they happen.

climatekids.nasa.gov/tidal-energy/
Learn about tidal power.

www.bbc.co.uk/nature/habitats/Coast
Learn about coastal habitats on this BBC site.

CLIPS

www.bbc.co.uk/education/clips/z7fr87h
Watch waves erode a cliff.

www.bbc.co.uk/education/clips/zbqhyrd
Discover how beaches form.

video.nationalgeographic.com/video/short-film-showcase/a-hypnotic-journey-through-waves-and-water
A journey through waves and water.

video.nationalgeographic.com/video/oceans-narrated-by-sylvia-earle/oceans-barrier-reef
Discover the wonders of the Great Barrier Reef.

wwwyoutube.com/watch?v=IlrqyHIE4wc
Check out Garrett McNamara's whopper-wave surfing.

wwwyoutube.com/watch?v=uX-_9IEiFSg
Listen to sand dunes sing!

INDEX